Christmas Carol Songbook

Words to all the holiday tunes you love plus tasty recipes &
tips to make your Christmas caroling party a big success

Winding Path Press

DEDICATION

This book is dedicated to Todd Edwards and all the family and friends (past and present) who have made Christmas Caroling such a fun and meaningful part of my holiday celebrations.

CONTENTS

Preface   vii

1   Tips for a Successful Caroling Party   1

2   Carols

     Angels We Have Heard on High   6

     The First Noel   8

     God Rest Ye, Merry Gentlemen   10

     Away In a Manger   13

     Good King Wenceslaus   14

     Hark, the Herald Angels Sing   16

     I Heard the Bells on Christmas Day   18

     It Came Upon the Midnight Clear   20

     Jingle Bells   22

     Joy to the World   24

     Here We Come A-Wassailing   26

     O Christmas Tree (O Tannenbaum)   29

     O Come All Ye Faithful   30

     O Holy Night   32

     O Little Town of Bethlehem   34

     Silent Night   36

The Twelve Days of Christmas   37

We Three Kings   40

We Wish You a Merry Christmas   42

The Snow Lay on the Ground   44

Deck the Halls   46

Good Christian Men Rejoice   48

Up On the Housetop   50

What Child is This   52

3 Recipes   55

    Appetizers   57

    Sweets   65

    Beverages   66

Preface

I co-hosted my first Christmas Caroling event when I was still in junior high school. I don't remember how it came about, but my friend Todd Edwards and I arranged it together. Everyone met at my house for "rehearsal" before heading out; and after caroling, we ended up at Todd's house where his mother had an array of delicious holiday goodies waiting for us.

We continued this tradition for several years, even after Todd and I didn't really hang out together anymore. In high school, the crowd got rowdier and it was always fun.

Then I remember hosting a couple of these parties alone when I was home from college and during my twenties, after Todd and I had lost touch. But the tradition eventually faded as I got older and my circle of friends changed.

Then I moved to Edinburg, Virginia, a town straight out of a Currier and Ives print and the tradition has been revived.

So I make this humble offering for my friends and family and anyone else who wants to enrich their holiday season with experiences other than shopping and wrapping and wondering how to pay for it all. These songs are all in the public domain so feel free to make copies for your guests to use. The large print makes for easier nighttime singing. I find that while everyone knows the tune, there is often a little disagreement on the words.

The recipes in this book are the same ones I use and the tips come from my own personal experience 'herding cats'.

Jeanne Russell
Publisher, Winding Path Press

TIPS FOR A SUCCESSFUL CAROLING PARTY

Hosting a successful caroling party is very much like hosting any other party; you want to arrange things so that your guests have fun and hopefully, so you have fun too. A caroling party, however, poses a couple of extra challenges because as the host you will essentially be "herding cats". And if you've never experienced this phenomena with cats or people, believe me, it can be quite frustrating.

It might go something like this. Everyone is assembled and you want to go over a couple of carols before heading out. Leila is in the middle of her story about her recent DMV experience and you can't get her attention. Jeffery whines that he doesn't see why everyone has to go out and sing to strangers anyway. Why can't we just have another glass of wine and forget the whole thing? Denise, who has already had several glasses of wine, insists on singing at the top of her lungs even though you haven't started rehearsal yet. Meanwhile the people who *were* ready to listen and start practice, have lost interest and wandered back to the food table and started new conversations. Jenny, who has been ready to sing since she arrived, complains that *no one is paying attention*! And Julia thinks it is too cold to go caroling. She's wearing her dress shoes and doesn't want them ruined. Some people are looking over the lyrics and practicing in small groups – of course each group is singing a different song and no one is listening to you.

Now at this point you might be to tempted to scream "Shut the F#@$ up!" and I have to admit that in the past I have resorted to raising my voice at these gatherings. But remember, you want everyone to have a good time; so maybe there is a different way to go. I've found that with a little forethought and preparation, one can forestall many of the problems that might otherwise ruin a Christmas Caroling party.

Here's a list of tips gleaned from my years of making mistakes. They will help you make your caroling party the event of the season.

Advice for the caroling part:

1. Make sure that you establish up front that this is a *Caroling* Party. Anyone not interested in singing should decline the invitation. That said, you should also stress that a lovely singing voice is not required.
2. Ask people to dress for the weather. You might think that when you tell people that they will be Christmas Caroling, they will automatically dress appropriately – not so. You need to remind them that they will be outside for longer then it takes to walk from their car to the house. Ask them to dress as if they were going sledding.
3. Recruit a friend to be the choir master for the evening. This person will announce the songs and decide when it is time to move on to the next house. Direct people with requests to make them to this person. Don't try to be the choir master yourself, you'll be too busy.
4. Sing through the songs while you're still at your house and agree ahead of time on which tune you'll be using for songs that have several versions (like *Away in a Manger*) and how many verses will be sung for each tune.
5. Establish a route and protocol. For example, you might decide to sing the first two verses of two carols at each house unless the listeners really seem to enjoy it, in which case you'll sing three.
6. Ask people to bring flashlights and have some on hand for when they forget.

Advice for the party:

1. Don't put all the food out at once. Save some for when you get back from the caroling. Everyone will have worked up an appetite by then and you want to be able to delight them with more and different treats.
2. Designate a "drunk sitter". You might decide not to serve alcohol at your caroling party, in which case you won't need this help. But if you decide to serve alcohol you want to designate a responsible friend to watch out for anyone who goes overboard on the holiday cheer. Even if your friends never drink too much, you should be prepared. There is something about the stress of the holidays that can cause even a normally sober person to overdo things. The drunk sitter can keep them safe and also keep them from disrupting the caroling too much.

THE CAROLS

Angels We Have Heard on High

Traditional French carol known as *Les Anges dans nos campagnes*
translated into English in 1862 by James Chadwick

Angels we have on heard high
Sweetly singing ore the plains
And the mountains in reply
Echoing their joyous strains

Gloria in excelsis Deo
Gloria in excelsis Deo

Come to Bethlehem and see
Christ whose birth the angels sing
Come adore on bended knee
Christ the Lord the newborn King

Gloria in excelsis Deo
Gloria in excelsis Deo

See him in a manger laid
Whom the choirs of angels praise
Mary, Joseph, lend your aid
While our hearts in love we raise

Gloria in excelsis Deo
Gloria, in excelsis Deo
Gloria in excelsis Deo

The First Noel
Author Unknown

The First Noel, the Angels did say
Was to certain poor shepherds in fields as they lay
In fields where they lay keeping their sheep
On a cold winter's night that was so deep.
Noel, Noel, Noel, Noel
Born is the King of Israel!

They looked up and saw a star
Shining in the East beyond them far
And to the earth it gave great light
And so it continued both day and night.
Noel, Noel, Noel, Noel
Born is the King of Israel!

And by the light of that same star
Three Wise men came from country far
To seek for a King was their intent
And to follow the star wherever it went.
Noel, Noel, Noel, Noel
Born is the King of Israel!

This star drew nigh to the northwest
O'er Bethlehem it took its rest

And there it did both Pause and stay
Right o'er the place where Jesus lay.
Noel, Noel, Noel, Noel
Born is the King of Israel!

Then entered in those Wise men three
Full reverently upon their knee
And offered there in His presence
Their gold and myrrh and frankincense.
Noel, Noel, Noel, Noel
Born is the King of Israel!

Then let us all with one accord
Sing praises to our heavenly Lord
That hath made Heaven and earth of naught
And with his blood mankind has bought.
Noel, Noel, Noel, Noel
Born is the King of Israel!

God Rest Ye, Merry Gentlemen

Author Unknown

God rest ye merry, gentlemen
Let nothing you dismay
Remember, Christ, our Savior
Was born on Christmas day
To save us all from Satan's power
When we were gone astray
O tidings of comfort and joy,
Comfort and joy
O tidings of comfort and joy

In Bethlehem, in Israel,
This blessed Babe was born
And laid within a manger
Upon this blessed morn
The which His Mother Mary
Did nothing take in scorn
O tidings of comfort and joy,
Comfort and joy
O tidings of comfort and joy

From God our Heavenly Father
A blessed Angel came;
And unto certain Shepherds

Brought tidings of the same:
How that in Bethlehem was born
The Son of God by Name.
O tidings of comfort and joy,
Comfort and joy
O tidings of comfort and joy

"Fear not then," said the Angel,
"Let nothing you affright,
This day is born a Savoir
Of a pure Virgin bright,
To free all those who trust in Him
From Satan's power and might."
O tidings of comfort and joy,
Comfort and joy
O tidings of comfort and joy

The shepherds at those tidings
Rejoiced much in mind,
And left their flocks a-feeding
In tempest, storm and wind:
And went to Bethlehem straightway
The Son of God to find.
O tidings of comfort and joy,
Comfort and joy
O tidings of comfort and joy

And when they came to Bethlehem
Where our dear Savoir lay,
They found Him in a manger,
Where oxen feed on hay;
His Mother Mary kneeling down,
Unto the Lord did pray.
O tidings of comfort and joy,
Comfort and joy
O tidings of comfort and joy

Now to the Lord sing praises,
All you within this place,
And with true love and brotherhood
Each other now embrace;
This holy tide of Christmas
All other doth deface.
O tidings of comfort and joy,
Comfort and joy
O tidings of comfort and jo

Away In a Manger

Author Unknown

Away in a manger,
No crib for His bed
The little Lord Jesus
Laid down His sweet head

The stars in the bright sky
Looked down where He lay
The little Lord Jesus
Asleep on the hay

The cattle are lowing
The poor Baby wakes
But little Lord Jesus
No crying He makes

I love Thee, Lord Jesus
Look down from the sky
And stay by my side,
'Til morning is nigh.

Bless all the dear children
In Thy tender care
And take us to heaven
To live with Thee there

Good King Wenceslaus

Words by John Mason Neale

Good King Wenceslas looked out
On the feast of Stephen
When the snow lay round about
Deep and crisp and even
Brightly shone the moon that night
Though the frost was cruel
When a poor man came in sight
Gath'ring winter fuel

"Hither, page, and stand by me
If thou know'st it, telling
Yonder peasant, who is he?
Where and what his dwelling?"
"Sire, he lives a good league hence
Underneath the mountain
Right against the forest fence
By Saint Agnes' fountain."

"Bring me flesh and bring me wine
Bring me pine logs hither
Thou and I will see him dine
When we bear him thither."
Page and monarch forth they went

Forth they went together
Through the rude wind's wild lament
And the bitter weather

"Sire, the night is darker now
And the wind blows stronger
Fails my heart, I know not how,
I can go no longer."
"Mark my footsteps, my good page
Tread thou in them boldly
Thou shalt find the winter's rage
Freeze thy blood less coldly."

In his master's steps he trod
Where the snow lay dinted
Heat was in the very sod
Which the Saint had printed
Therefore, Christian men, be sure
Wealth or rank possessing
Ye who now will bless the poor
Shall yourselves find blessing

Hark, the Herald Angels Sing

By Charles Wesley

Hark the herald angels sing
"Glory to the newborn King!
Peace on earth and mercy mild
God and sinners reconciled"
Joyful, all ye nations rise
Join the triumph of the skies
With the angelic host proclaim:
"Christ is born in Bethlehem"
Hark! The herald angels sing
"Glory to the newborn King!"

Christ by highest heaven adored
Christ the everlasting Lord!
Late in time behold Him come
Offspring of a Virgin's womb
Veiled in flesh the Godhead see
Hail the incarnate Deity
Pleased as man with man to dwell
Jesus, our Emmanuel
Hark! The herald angels sing
"Glory to the newborn King!"

Hail the heav'n-born Prince of Peace!
Hail the Son of Righteousness!
Light and life to all He brings
Ris'n with healing in His wings
Mild He lays His glory by
Born that man no more may die
Born to raise the sons of earth
Born to give them second birth
Hark! The herald angels sing
"Glory to the newborn King!"

I Heard the Bells on Christmas Day

Henry Wadsworth Longfellow 1867

I Heard the Bells on Christmas Day
Their old familiar carols play,
And wild and sweet the words repeat
Of peace on earth, good will to men.

I thought how, as the day had come,
The belfries of all Christendom
Had rolled along the unbroken song
Of peace on earth, good will to men.

And in despair I bowed my head:
"There is no peace on earth," I said,
"For hate is strong and mocks the song
Of peace on earth, good will to men."

Then pealed the bells more loud and deep:
"God is not dead, nor doth he sleep;
The wrong shall fail, the right prevail,
With peace on earth, good will to men."

Till, ringing singing, on its way,
The world revolved from night to day,
A voice, a chime, a chant sublime,
Of peace on earth, good will to men!

It Came Upon the Midnight Clear

Edmund Sears, 1849

It came upon the midnight clear,
That glorious song of old,
From angels bending near the earth,
To touch their harps of gold:
"Peace on the earth, goodwill to men
From heavens all gracious King!"
The world in solemn stillness lay
To hear the angels sing.

Still through the cloven skies they come,
With peaceful wings unfurled;
And still their heavenly music floats
O'er all the weary world:
Above its sad and lowly plains
They bend on hovering wing,
And ever o'er its Babel sounds
The blessed angels sing.

O ye beneath life's crushing load,
Whose forms are bending low,
Who toil along the climbing way
With painful steps and slow;
Look now, for glad and golden hours

Come swiftly on the wing;
Oh rest beside the weary road
And hear the angels sing.

For lo! the days are hastening on,
By prophets seen of old,
When with the ever-circling years
Shall come the time foretold,
When the new heaven and earth shall own
The Prince of Peace, their King,
And the whole world send back the song
Which now the angels sing.

Jingle Bells

James Pierpoint, 1857

Dashing through the snow
On a one-horse open sleigh,
O'er the fields we go,
Laughing all the way;
Bells on bob-tail ring,
Making spirits bright,
What fun it is to ride and sing
A sleighing song tonight
Jingle bells, jingle bells,
Jingle all the way!
O what fun it is to ride
In a one-horse open sleigh

A day or two ago,
I thought I'd take a ride,
And soon Miss Fanny Bright
Was seated by my side;
The horse was lean and lank;
Misfortune seemed his lot;
He got into a drifted bank,
And we, we got upsot.
Jingle Bells, Jingle Bells,
Jingle all the way!

What fun it is to ride
In a one-horse open sleigh.

Now the ground is white
Go it while you're young,
Take the girls tonight
And sing this sleighing song;
Just get a bob-tailed bay
Two-forty as his speed
Hitch him to an open sleigh
And crack! you'll take the lead.
Jingle Bells, Jingle Bells,
Jingle all the way!
What fun it is to ride
In a one-horse open sleigh.

Joy to the World

Words by Isaac Watts

Joy to the world, the Lord is come!
Let earth receive her King;
Let every heart prepare Him room,
And Heaven and nature sing,
And Heaven and nature sing,
And Heaven, and Heaven, and nature sing.

Joy to the earth, the Savior reigns!
Let men their songs employ;
While fields and floods, rocks, hills and plains
Repeat the sounding joy,
Repeat the sounding joy,
Repeat, repeat, the sounding joy.

No more let sins and sorrows grow,
Nor thorns infest the ground;
He comes to make His blessings flow
Far as the curse is found,
Far as the curse is found,
Far as, far as, the curse is found.

He rules the world with truth and grace,
And makes the nations prove
The glories of His righteousness,
And wonders of His love,
And wonders of His love,
And wonders, wonders, of His love.

Here We Come A-Wassailing

Here we come a-wassailing
Among the leaves so green,
Here we come a-wandering
So fair to be seen.
Love and joy come to you,
And to you your wassail, too,
And God bless you, and send you
A Happy New Year,
And God send you a Happy New Year.

We are not daily beggars
That beg from door to door,
But we are neighbors' children
Whom you have seen before
Love and joy come to you,
And to you your wassail, too,
And God bless you, and send you
A Happy New Year,
And God send you a Happy New Year.

Good master and good mistress,
As you sit beside the fire,
Pray think of us poor children
Who wander in the mire.
Love and joy come to you,
And to you your wassail, too,
And God bless you, and send you
A Happy New Year,
And God send you a Happy New Year.

Bring us out a table
And spread it with a cloth;
Bring us out a cheese,
And of your Christmas loaf.
Love and joy come to you,
And to you your wassail, too,
And God bless you, and send you
A Happy New Year,
And God send you a Happy New Year.

God bless the master of this house,
Likewise the mistress too;
And all the little children
That round the table go.
Love and joy come to you,
And to you your wassail, too,
And God bless you, and send you
A Happy New Year,
And God send you a Happy New Year.

O Christmas Tree (O Tannenbaum)
Original words by Ernst Gebhard Anschütz

O Christmas Tree, O Christmas Tree,
Your branches green delight us!
They're green when summer days are bright,
They're green when winter snow is white.
O Christmas Tree, O Christmas Tree,
Your branches green delight us!

O Christmas Tree, O Christmas Tree,
You give us so much pleasure!
How oft at Christmas tide the sight,
O green fir tree, gives us delight!
O Christmas Tree, O Christmas Tree,
You give us so much pleasure!

O Christmas Tree, O Christmas Tree
You fill my heart with music.
Reminding me on Christmas Day
To think of you and then be gay.
O Christmas Tree, O Christmas Tree
You fill my heart with music.

O Come All Ye Faithful

Words by John Wade

O come, all ye faithful, joyful and triumphant,
O come ye, O come ye, to Bethlehem.
Come and behold Him, born the King of angels;

O come, let us adore Him,
O come, let us adore Him,
O come, let us adore Him,
Christ the Lord.

True God of true God, Light from Light Eternal,
Lo, He shuns not the Virgin's womb;
Son of the Father, begotten, not created;

O come, let us adore Him,
O come, let us adore Him,
O come, let us adore Him,
Christ the Lord

Sing, choirs of angels, sing in exultation;
O sing, all ye citizens of heaven above!
Glory to God, all glory in the highest;

O come, let us adore Him,
O come, let us adore Him,
O come, let us adore Him,
Christ the Lord

Lo! star led chieftains, Magi, Christ adoring,
Offer Him incense, gold, and myrrh;
We to the Christ Child bring our hearts' oblations.

O come, let us adore Him,
O come, let us adore Him,
O come, let us adore Him,
Christ the Lord

Child, for us sinners poor and in the manger,
We would embrace Thee, with love and awe;
Who would not love Thee, loving us so dearly?

O come, let us adore Him,
O come, let us adore Him,
O come, let us adore Him,
Christ the Lord

Yea, Lord, we greet Thee, born this happy
morning;
Jesus, to Thee be glory given;
Word of the Father, now in flesh appearing.

O come, let us adore Him,
O come, let us adore Him,
O come, let us adore Him,
Christ the Lord

O Holy Night

English lyrics by John Sullivan Dwight, based on original French poem by Placide Cappeau

O Holy Night
The stars are brightly shining
It is the night of our dear Savior's birth
Long lay the world in sin and error pining
Till he appeared
And the soul felt it's worth
The thrill of hope
The weary world rejoices
For yonder brinks a new and glorious morn
Fall on your knees
O hear the angel voices
O night divine
O night when Christ was born
O night divine
O night, o night divine

O Holy Night
The stars are brightly shining
It is the night of our dear Savior's birth
Long lay the world
In sin and error-pining
Till he appeared
And the soul felt it's worth
The thrill of hope
The weary world rejoices
For yonder brinks
A new and glorious morn
Fall on your knees

O hear the angel voices
O night divine
O night when Christ was born
O night divine
O night, o night divine

O Little Town of Bethlehem

Words by Phillips Brooks

O little town of Bethlehem
How still we see thee lie
Above thy deep and dreamless sleep
The silent stars go by
Yet in thy dark streets shineth
The everlasting Light
The hopes and fears of all the years
Are met in thee tonight

For Christ is born of Mary
And gathered all above
While mortals sleep, the angels keep
Their watch of wondering love
O morning stars together
Proclaim the holy birth
And praises sing to God the King
And Peace to men on earth

How silently, how silently
The wondrous gift is given!
So God imparts to human hearts
The blessings of His heaven.
No ear may his His coming,

But in this world of sin,
Where meek souls will receive him still,
The dear Christ enters in.

O holy Child of Bethlehem
Descend to us, we pray
Cast out our sin and enter in
Be born to us today
We hear the Christmas angels
The great glad tidings tell
O come to us, abide with us
Our Lord Emmanuel

Silent Night

Words by Josef Mohr

Silent night, holy night
All is calm, all is bright
Round yon Virgin Mother and Child
Holy Infant so tender and mild
Sleep in heavenly peace
Sleep in heavenly peace

Silent night, holy night!
Shepherds quake at the sight
Glories stream from heaven afar
Heavenly hosts sing Alleluia!
Christ, the Saviour is born
Christ, the Saviour is born

Silent night, holy night
Son of God, love's pure light
Radiant beams from Thy holy face
With the dawn of redeeming grace
Jesus, Lord, at Thy birth
Jesus, Lord, at Thy birth "

The Twelve Days of Christmas

Author Unknown

On the **first** day of Christmas
my true love sent to me:
A Partridge in a Pear Tree

On the **second** day of Christmas
my true love sent to me:
Two Turtle Doves
and a Partridge in a Pear Tree

On the **third** day of Christmas
my true love sent to me:
Three French Hens
Two Turtle Doves
and a Partridge in a Pear Tree

On the **fourth** day of Christmas
my true love sent to me:
Four Calling Birds*
Three French Hens
Two Turtle Doves
and a Partridge in a Pear Tree

On the **fifth** day of Christmas
my true love sent to me:
Five Golden Rings
Four Calling Birds
Three French Hens
Two Turtle Doves
and a Partridge in a Pear Tree

On the **sixth** day of Christmas
my true love sent to me:
Six Geese a Laying
Five Golden Rings
Four Calling Birds
Three French Hens
Two Turtle Doves
and a Partridge in a Pear Tree

On the **seventh** day of Christmas
my true love sent to me:
Seven Swans a Swimming

Six Geese a Laying
Five Golden Rings
Four Calling Birds
Three French Hens
Two Turtle Doves
and a Partridge in a Pear
Tree

On the **eighth** day of
Christmas
my true love sent to me:
Eight Maids a Milking
Seven Swans a
Swimming
Six Geese a Laying
Five Golden Rings
Four Calling Birds
Three French Hens
Two Turtle Doves
and a Partridge in a Pear
Tree

On the **ninth** day of
Christmas
my true love sent to me:
Nine Ladies Dancing
Eight Maids a Milking
Seven Swans a
Swimming
Six Geese a Laying
Five Golden Rings
Four Calling Birds

Three French Hens
Two Turtle Doves
and a Partridge in a Pear
Tree

On the **tenth** day of
Christmas
my true love sent to me:
Ten Lords a Leaping
Nine Ladies Dancing
Eight Maids a Milking
Seven Swans a
Swimming
Six Geese a Laying
Five Golden Rings
Four Calling Birds
Three French Hens
Two Turtle Doves
and a Partridge in a Pear
Tree

On the **eleventh** day of
Christmas
my true love sent to me:
Eleven Pipers Piping
Ten Lords a Leaping
Nine Ladies Dancing
Eight Maids a Milking
Seven Swans a
Swimming
Six Geese a Laying
Five Golden Rings

Four Calling Birds
Three French Hens
Two Turtle Doves

and a Partridge in a Pear
Tree

On the **twelfth** day of
Christmas
my true love sent to me:
12 Drummers
Drumming
Eleven Pipers Piping
Ten Lords a Leaping
Nine Ladies Dancing
Eight Maids a Milking
Seven Swans a
Swimming
Six Geese a Laying
Five Golden Rings
Four Calling Birds
Three French Hens
Two Turtle Doves
and a Partridge in a Pear
Tree

We Three Kings

By John Henry Hopkins, Jr.

We three kings of Orient are
Bearing gifts we traverse afar
Field and fountain, moor and mountain
Following yonder star

O Star of wonder, star of night
Star with royal beauty bright
Westward leading, still proceeding
Guide us to thy Perfect Light

Born a King on Bethlehem's plain
Gold I bring to crown Him again
King forever, ceasing never
Over us all to rein

O Star of wonder, star of night
Star with royal beauty bright
Westward leading, still proceeding
Guide us to Thy perfect light

Frankincense to offer have I
Incense owns a Deity nigh

Prayer and praising, all men raising
Worship Him, God most high

O Star of wonder, star of night
Star with royal beauty bright
Westward leading, still proceeding
Guide us to Thy perfect light

Myrrh is mine, its bitter perfume
Breathes of life of gathering gloom
Sorrowing, sighing, bleeding, dying
Sealed in the stone-cold tomb

O Star of wonder, star of night
Star with royal beauty bright
Westward leading, still proceeding
Guide us to Thy perfect light

Glorious now behold Him arise
King and God and Sacrifice
Alleluia, Alleluia
Earth to heav'n replies

O Star of wonder, star of night...

We Wish You a Merry Christmas

Arthur Unknown

We wish you a merry Christmas
We wish you a merry Christmas
We wish you a merry Christmas
And a happy New Year.
Glad tidings we bring
To you and your kin;
Glad tidings for Christmas
And a happy New Year!

We want some figgy pudding
We want some figgy pudding
We want some figgy pudding
Please bring it right here!
Glad tidings we bring
To you and your kin;
Glad tidings for Christmas
And a happy New Year!

We won't go until we get some
We won't go until we get some
We won't go until we get some
So bring it out here!
Glad tidings we bring
To you and your kin;
Glad tidings for Christmas
And a happy New Year!

We wish you a Merry Christmas
We wish you a Merry Christmas

We wish you a Merry Christmas
And a happy New Year.
Glad tidings we bring

The Snow Lay on the Ground
Traditional Irish Carol

The snow lay on the ground, the star shone bright,
When Christ our Lord was born, On Christmas
night.

Venite adoremus Dominum;
Venite adoremus Dominum;
Venite adoremus Dominum;
Venite adoremus Dominum.

'Twas Mary, Virgin pure, Of holy Anne,
That brought into this world the God made man.
She laid Him in a stall At Bethlehem,
The ass and oxen share the roof with them.

Venite adoremus Dominum;
Venite adoremus Dominum.

Saint Joseph, too, was by To tend the child;
To guard Him and protect His Mother mild;
The angels hovered round And sang this song:

Venite adoremus Dominum;

Venite adoremus Dominum;
Venite adoremus Dominum.
And, thus, that manger poor became a throne;
For He whom Mary bore was God the Son.
O come then, let us join the heavenly host,
To praise the Father, Son, and Holy Ghost.

Venite adoremus Dominum;
Venite adoremus Dominum.

Deck the Halls
Author Unknown

Deck the halls with boughs of holly,
Fa la la la la, la la la la.
Tis the season to be jolly,
Fa la la la la, la la la la.

Don we now our gay apparel,
Fa la la, la la la, la la la.
Troll the ancient Yule tide carol,
Fa la la la la, la la la la.

See the blazing Yule before us,
Fa la la la la, la la la la.
Strike the harp and join the chorus.
Fa la la la la, la la la la.

Follow me in merry measure,
Fa la la la la, la la la la.
While I tell of Yule tide treasure,
Fa la la la la, la la la la.

Fast away the old year passes,
Fa la la la la, la la la la.

Hail the new, ye lads and lasses,
Fa la la la la, la la la la.

Sing we joyous, all together,
Fa la la la la, la la la la.
Heedless of the wind and weather,
Fa la la la la, la la la la.

Good Christian Men Rejoice

Words by Heinrich Suso and translated into English by John Mason Neale

Good Christian men rejoice
With heart and soul and voice!
Give ye heed to what we say
(News! News!)
Jesus Christ is born today!
Ox and ass before Him bow
And He is in the manger now
Christ is born today!
Christ is born today!

Good Christian men, rejoice
With heart and soul and voice
Now ye hear of endless bliss
(Joy! Joy!)
Jesus Christ was born for this
He hath open'd the heav'nly door
And man is blessed evermore
Christ was born for this
Christ was born for this

Good Christian men, rejoice
With heart and soul and voice

Now ye need not fear the grave:

(Peace! Peace!)

Jesus Christ was born to save

Calls you one and calls you all

To gain His everlasting hall

Christ was born to save

Christ was born to save

Winding Path Press

Up On the Housetop

by Benjamin Hanby

Up on the housetop reindeer pause
Out jumps good old Santa Claus
Down through the chimney with lots of toys
All for the little ones, Christmas joys
Ho, ho ho! Who wouldn't go? Ho, ho ho! Who
wouldn't go?

Up on the housetop, click, click, click
Down through the chimney with old Saint Nick

First comes the stocking of little Nell
Oh, dear Santa fill it well
Give her a dolly that laughs and cries
One that will open and shut her eyes
Ho, ho, ho! Who wouldn't go? Ho, ho, ho! Who
wouldn't go?

Up on the housetop, click, click, click
Down through the chimney with old Saint Nick

Next comes the stocking of little Will
Oh, just see what a glorious fill
Here is a hammer and lots of tacks

Also a ball and a whip that cracks
Ho, ho ho! Who wouldn't go? Ho, ho, ho! Who
wouldn't go?

Up on the housetop, click, click, click
Down through the chimney with old Saint Nick

What Child is This
Words by William Chatterton Dix

What Child is this who, laid to rest
On Mary's lap is sleeping?
Whom Angels greet with anthems sweet,
While shepherds watch are keeping?

This, this is Christ the King,
Whom shepherds guard and Angels sing;
Haste, haste, to bring Him laud,
The Babe, the Son of Mary.

Why lies He in such mean estate,
Where ox and ass are feeding?
Good Christians, fear, for sinners here
The silent Word is pleading.

Nails, spear shall pierce Him through,
The cross be borne for me, for you.
Hail, hail the Word made flesh,
The Babe, the Son of Mary.

So bring Him incense, gold and myrrh,
Come peasant, king to own Him;
The King of kings salvation brings,
Let loving hearts enthrone Him.

Raise, raise a song on high,
The virgin sings her lullaby.
Joy, joy for Christ is born,
The Babe, the Son of Mary.

Recipes for your Holiday Parties

Party Food

When entertaining for the holidays, you want to serve food that is tasty, pretty, easy to make, and that accommodates the different tastes and dietary restrictions of your guests.

The following recipes are ones I've served at my Christmas caroling parties with great success. They cover a variety of palettes, from meat lovers to vegetarians, to gluten-free. Please bear in mind that I never measure ingredients unless it is absolutely necessary so the measurements indicated are approximate - feel free to alter these recipes to your own tastes.

"Trust thyself, every heart vibrates to that iron tone."

– Ralph Waldo Emerson

 Indicates a recipe that is Gluten-free (or that could be gluten-free)

 Indicates vegetarian recipe

Christmas Tree Appetizer

1 pkg crescent rolls
1 tub whipped cream cheese
1 clove fresh garlic (crushed)
½ tsp dill weed
¼ tsp onion salt
2 or 3 sprigs fresh broccoli (chopped)
1 small red bell pepper (chopped)
1 large mushroom (chopped)
½ cucumber (deseeded and chopped)
1 small carrot (chopped)
other chopped fresh veggies as desired

Preheat oven to 375°. Open crescent rolls and slice log into 16 rounds using a very sharp knife or dental floss. Arrange circles on a rectangular stone or baking sheet in the shape of a Christmas Tree as follows: Shape one circle into a square by pushing in the sides. This will be your tree trunk. Above this place a row of 5 circles side by side for the bottom row. Center 4 circles above that, three above that and so on. It will look like this:

Put this in the oven and bake until golden brown (about 10 minutes). Remove and let cool. While the crescent tree is cooling, prepare the other ingredients. In a small bowl mix cream cheese, garlic, dill weed, and onion salt. Set aside. Now chop your vegetables. You will be using the broccoli as the green fir needles, the mushroom as bark, and everything else for decorations. When the crescent tree has cooled, spread cream cheese mixture on entire surface. Use mushroom to create the bark on the tree trunk. Sprinkle the rest of the tree with chopped broccoli and then use remaining vegetables to decorate the tree. This makes a tasty and festive treat.

Baked Artichoke Dip

1 15 oz can artichoke hearts (quartered)
1 package shredded parmesan cheese
¼ cup real mayonnaise
1 clove garlic (crushed)
Paprika

Preheat oven to 375°. Mix artichoke hearts, cheese, mayonnaise and garlic in a glass or stone pie pan. Sprinkle with paprika and bake until bubbly. Serve with French bread rounds or gluten free crackers.

Sausage Cheese Balls

1 package hot sausage (1 lb)
1 big hunk of sharp cheddar cheese (shredded)
1 Small box of Bisquick ™ (20 oz)

Preheat oven to 375° In large bowl mix all ingredients. You're going to have to use your hands to get everything to get all the dry parts mixed in to form a dough. Form dough into 1 inch balls, place on baking sheet and cook until done. This will take 30 to 35 minutes. It is important to cook thoroughly. The balls will be golden outside and done on the inside.

Bacon Pineapple

1 fresh pineapple cut into ¾ inch chunks
1 jar chili sauce
1 package bacon
¼ to ½ cup brown sugar
Dash of cayenne pepper hot sauce
Toothpicks for serving

Preheat oven to 375°. Cut bacon slices in half. Wrap each pineapple chunk with bacon and place in shallow baking dish. Bake until bacon is crisp (about 35 minutes but it varies). Meanwhile in a small saucepan combine chili sauce, brown sugar and hot pepper sauce and heat until sugar is dissolved. Keep warm until bacon/pineapple chunks are done. Transfer chunks to serving dish and pour chili sauce mixture over chunks. Serve with little forks or toothpicks.

Deviled Eggs

1 dozen hard boiled eggs
¼ cup chopped pickles (bread and butter best)
2 TBS apple cider vinegar
1 TBS spicy brown mustard
2 TBS Mayonnaise
Salt and pepper to taste
Paprika

Slice hard boiled eggs in half, place whites on tray and yolks in bowl. Add chopped pickles, vinegar, mustard, mayonnaise and salt and pepper to yolks. Mix well. Scoop yolk mixture into egg white shells or pipe using a pastry bag. Sprinkle with paprika.

Sweet Potato Appetizer

2 sweet potatoes
¼ cup olive oil
1 tsp onion salt
Sour cream for dipping

Preheat oven to 375°. Slice sweet potatoes into wedges. Mix onion salt, olive oil and potatoes until potatoes are evenly covered. (Depending on the size of your sweet potatoes, you might need more oil and onion salt.) Spread out in large stone baking dish and cook for about 45 minutes (basting potatoes periodically as needed). Serve with sour cream.

Cilantro Dip with Rice Cubes

1 cup long grain rice
5 cups water

1 bunch chopped cilantro
3 or 4 scallions (chopped)
The juice of 1 lemon
2 cloves garlic
1 small red chili pepper (chopped)
¼ cup peanut butter
3 TBS Coconut milk
Coarsely ground black pepper
White pepper to taste
Salt

Make rice cubes a day ahead. Cook rice with 5 cups water. It will be sticky and moist. Scoop ¼ to 1/3 of the cooked rice into the food processor and grind. Mix this back into the rest of the rice and then spread out into a pan you have lined with parchment paper. Spread plastic wrap over the top, cover with something heavy and put in the refrigerator to set. The next day, you will remove plastic wrap, turn onto a cutting board, peal off parchment paper then cut with sharp knife that has been dipped in water. Cut into cubes and arrange cubes on a tray. These cubes will be dipped into cilantro sauce.

To make sauce: Process cilantro, scallions, chili pepper and garlic. Add peanut butter, coconut milk, lemon juice, salt and pepper. (Be generous with the salt and pepper.) and process until smooth. Transfer to a small sauce pan, bring to boil, reduce heat and cook a few more minutes. Let cool. This can be made ahead and stored in the refrigerator for a couple of days. If it seems too thick, add more lemon juice and/or water and stir.

Ginger Garlic Chicken Wings

1 package chicken wings
1 big chunk of fresh ginger pealed and chopped.
5 or more cloves of garlic peeled and chopped
Cayenne pepper hot sauce (Lots)
Olive oil
Salt and pepper

Coat large iron skillet or wok with olive oil. Sprinkle salt and pepper on wings and then cook on high heat turning frequently until browned. Add garlic, ginger and hot sauce. Lower heat and cover, stirring and scrapping pan frequently until wings are cooked through. Serve hot. Yum!

Pesto Goat Cheese on celery (or garlic French bread rounds)

(I got the original version of this from my friend Jody Steiner-Kelly.)

1 pkg goat cheese, crumbled
pesto sauce (either homemade or packaged)
¼ chopped sun dried tomatoes or regular tomatoes (sans seeds)
1 bunch celery (for gluten-free version)
Or 1 loaf French bread, olive oil, and 1 clove crushed fresh garlic

For gluten free version: wash celery and cut into serving sized pieces. Set aside.

For gluten-ful version: slice French bread, place on baking stone and baste with olive oil/garlic mixture. Cook at 375° until slightly toasted. Set aside.

In small bowl, combine crumbled goat cheese with pesto and mix until it makes a creamy light green paste. Spread paste on celery stalks or bread rounds. Garnish tops with tomato pieces and arrange on platter.

Jeanne's Stuffed Mushrooms

1 pkg large mushrooms
3/4 cup grated sharp cheddar cheese
¾ cup crumbled feta
2 cloves crushed garlic
Salt and pepper
Red pepper flakes to taste
Paprika

Preheat oven to 375°. Wash and de-stem mushrooms reserving a few stems of the stems, Chop reserved stems and mix with cheddar, feta, garlic and red pepper flakes. Sprinkle salt and pepper on mushroom caps and fill with cheese mixture. Sprinkle with paprika and bak until bubbly.

Baked Queso dip

Grated Cheddar (3 cups or more)
1 Onion (Chopped)
1 Pepper (Chopped)
½ Cup salsa
½ cup milk or cream
Cayenne pepper sauce to taste

Place all ingredients in a shallow baking dish and bake at 350° for 20 minutes and then stir. Continue baking until bubbly. Serve with chips.

Cocoa-oatmeal Candy

2 cups sugar
3 TBS cocoa powder
½ tsp salt
1 stick butter
½ cup milk
½ cup peanut butter
4 ½ cups uncooked oatmeal
1 tsp vanilla

Mix sugar, cocoa, salt, butter, and milk in saucepan. Boil 2 minutes. Remove from heat and add peanut butter, oatmeal, and vanilla. Mix thoroughly; drop on waxed paper and let harden.

Bourdon balls

(From Alice Russell)

3 cups vanilla wafer crumbs (1 box)
1 cup powdered sugar
1 cup finely chopped pecans
11/2 TBS cocoa
3 TBS White Karo ™ syrup
3 ounces bourdon whiskey

Roll wafers into fine crumbs and combine with other ingredients to make a big glob. Pinch off bits and roll in hands to form small balls. Roll each ball in powdered sugar. Place in airtight container and allow to ripen for at least 3 days.

White chocolate chip cookies
(Recipe from Grandmom, Alice Micklem Maphis)

These cookies are to be made at night before you go to bed.

2 egg whites
¾ to 1 cup of sugar
 Pinch of salt
1 teaspoon vanilla
1 cup chopped nuts
1 cup semi-sweet chocolate chips

Preheat oven to 350° for 20 minutes. Beat egg white stiff. Gradually add sugar and salt. Keep beating until sugar is dissolved and mixture is still stiff. Fold in vanilla then nuts and chocolate chips. Drop on baking stone or greased cookie sheet. Turn oven off and place cookies in overnight.

Egg Nog
(Recipe from my mom, Alice Russell,
who got it from her mom and so on...)

1 dozen fresh eggs
1 quart brandy
Dash Rum (1/2 cup or more)
1 ½ quarts table cream
1 quart milk
¼ to ½ cup sugar

Separate eggs. Beat yellows. Slowly sitr in brandy and rum. Then slowly add cream and milk. Set aside. Beat egg whites until stiff. Slowly beat in sugar. Fold whites into yellow mixture. Pour into containers. My mom uses old wine carafes. Let mellow in the refrigerator at least 1 day – preferably two.

Mulled Wine

This recipe is good because of the lower alcohol content. An alternative stronger version can be made by omitting the apple juice and honey and using a sweet red wine in place of the dry.

1 part dry red wine
1 part apple juice
1 cinnamon stick
½ tsp allspice
1/2 tsp nutmeg
½ tsp cardamom
1 tsp cloves
Orange slice
Honey or guava nectar to taste

Pour wine and apple juice in crock pot (or you can use a saucepan on the stovetop). Place spices and orange slice in a square of cheese cloth and secure with string to create a loose bundle of spices. Heat slowly and serve to cold a thirsty guests.

Mulled Apple Cider

Same as above except replace apple juice with cider and omit the wine.

About Winding Path Press

Winding Path Press gets its' name from the Labyrinth in publisher, Jeanne Russell's backyard. That labyrinth was created with the help of dear friends and serves as a source of serenity and peace for those who choose to walk it.

Winding Path Press seeks publish books that promote community, introspection, and positive change – just Like the labyrinth.

To find out more about Winding Path Press, visit: www.windingpathpress.com

Made in the USA
Middletown, DE
16 December 2017